A BRIEF KISS WITH DEATH

Anna Maria Wilkison

A Brief Kiss With Death

The greatest love story ever told of an organ transplant caretaker, wife, and mother!

For those dealing with adversity, severe illness, and recovery.

This Book is dedicated to my Loving Husband and Beautiful daughter!

William Thomas Wilkison
&

Christine Marie Wilkison

Also known as Daddy & Moonpie

Table of Contents:

INTRODUCTION

On April 21st 2015 in the Sunny state of South Carolina a husband and wife were called into the doctor's office to receive news that would forever change their lives. I can still hear the words.... I am so sorry but your liver, your liver.... well you have cirrhosis. My husband and I sat there speechless thinking this can't be happening. On the long drive home, we were in separate vehicles and the highway drive was backed up with traffic, I felt it was the longest journey that I had ever taken in my life but little did I know what lied ahead. Sitting there trying to the process the unthinkable, I fixed my lipstick as if I could make the news seem better with a quick swipe of ruby red! You see I have always been accused of being somewhat of a perfectionist, in fact people would come to me for advice on how to make things better. I wish there was another me laying around to give me some of that advise today!

Notes:

TRYING TO PROCESS

I woke up every morning to an unfamiliar feeling of fatality! The pieces of this puzzle did not fit. The news of my husband's medical report was unbearable, unthinkable and undeniably unimaginable! In a nutshell it was just plain crazy! I quickly realized that all the restless nights and tear stained pillows didn't change or resolve one thing and besides, it just made my eyes look dark and puffy, which meant I had to use extra concealer the next day. I knew I had to hold us together! I would soon discover that third person would hold us down! Third person's first name was Anna and the last name was All-Day!

My third person and keen sense of survival was at an all-time high!

My daily conversations with God were heightened by my spiritual quest for direction. We may not always see our way through adversity with a natural eye, but God was revealing something so much more to me. The Lord said abide in me no matter how rocky the situation gets! Abide!

John 15:4 - Abide in me, and I in you. As the branch cannot bear fruit of itself unless it abides in the vine, so neither can you unless you abide in me.

Notes:

OUR LIFE BEFORE SICKNESS!

I thank my Lord and Savior every day for a beautiful family and a wonderful life. I have lived life on both sides of the dollar and it has always kept me humble no matter how many blessings came my way. I lived in many states and have been fortunate to be surrounded by the finer things in life. Fine homes, cars and a tremendous appetite for growth! We are a self-made couple that became out casts from our family and social groups. My husband's family disowned/disinherited him completely and it was made clear they would never accept an inter-racial marriage. Unfortunately, I didn't come from a tight knit family, which meant there were very few in my corner, but that's another book. Our love was considered by many to be taboo.

When my husband and I were together in the community we were constantly asked if we were together. One example is walking into a restaurant on my husband's arm and being asked would there be someone joining tonight Madam or will you be dining alone. I always politely answered table for two please but my inner voice screamed, "I'll dine alone just overlook the big 6'7" giant that I'm glued to". We were an inter- racial couple raising a biracial daughter it was a no no! We always understood what the odds were against us. We always looked out for each other and continued to grow our nest egg which became our security blanket. We didn't have others who believed in us or supported our dreams.

My husband stood 6'7", bald, ivory skin with hazel eyes. Our daughter was beautiful, ivory skin, 5'2", deep dark luxurious curls and a figure to die for. I am 5'8" with exotic facial features, shapely silhouette, with a stand out flare for fashion, former model/singer, ready to get my hands dirty on the drop of a dime, certified personal trainer, published Poet, and will always remain a true visionary.... now breathe. Never the less, we were determined to claim our space in the world. Our old-fashioned values on commitment, family, work ethic and school of hard Knox has laid a foundation of beating the odds while always remaining humble in the presence of God.

My clock was always set before anyone in their right mind would even think about getting up. Workouts, chores and long drives to and from our daughter's school every day. I wanted to make sure my family was well cared for and felt a warm sense of love from me.

Taking care of my heath and appearance was a top priority as well because when I felt good, it allowed me to give more of myself to what matters most......FAMILY!

Eventually our daughter grows up and hubby and I are empty nesters. We decided to buy a smaller home and start looking for a beach house. We were always making plans on what was next. There was never a moment of void in our lives. Always adventure! I always knew we were extraordinary together. We referred to our marital status as toe tags and body bags because we agreed that was the only way out of the marriage. How funny writing this and how it sounds out loud.......

Notes:

THE REFERRAL

We were referred to a Specialist who initially explained to us that he sees liver numbers like this all the time. The specialist also said he would keep an eye on the numbers and my husband's condition and liver numbers should improve over time. Unfortunately, his liver numbers continued to get worse along with the specialist's personal opinion that my husband's condition was being caused by all day alcohol use. No matter how many times my husband and I told him that was not the case we couldn't convince him otherwise. My husband was upfront from the start as he told him that alcohol was used socially but there was no all-day alcohol use or addiction. He also mentioned when he was first diagnosed with cirrhosis, alcohol was removed and all necessary changes in diet was made. This meant no alcohol and eating completely clean. Some of his medications were discontinued as well. The specialist was asked multiple times to test him for traces of alcohol if he felt that way. The specialist said that he didn't feel that was necessary because he knew what was going on.

He was hospitalized on multiple occasions at the local hospital where the specialist responded to calls. We had a male nurse mention that the specialist noted my husband's condition was self-induced by alcohol. I said that is false, as I explained his history and what had been taking place. The nurse asked a lot of personal questions about our history together. He told me he was a gay man living in the South and was judged very harshly by family & friends. The nurse also said I can imagine the discrimination and judgement you and your husband have faced. He said I'm not trying to be nosey but there are a lot of people in this hospital judging you and your husband, not just about the specialists notes but your relationship status. No one believes that you are his wife! Remember we are in the South and the whole inter-racial marriage or having a gay relationship is still judged very harshly in this area. I shook my head as I showed him my license and pointed out my last name. He said I am so sorry about your husband's condition and if there is anything you need while I'm here, then please ask for me personally. I thanked him as he left the room. It was getting late so I kissed my husband and told him I would see him bright and early the next morning. When I passed the nurses station on the way out, I overheard one of the nurses say to the other, "there goes the entertainment", as they both laughed hysterically. I now understood the poor treatment, disrespectful comments and smug stares. I began to pray not only for myself and my husband but for the ones that displayed so much hate. I also prayed for anyone that may have had an addiction. My thoughts are if we're in a position to make a difference, we need to ask ourselves as humans, are we here to hurt or to heal....... My voice was lost among scholars and drowned out by the personal opinions of those holding PHD's.

I prayed Dear God can you hear me crying on the inside. Can you hear me God?

Praise God! My tears dried and my steps were divinely ordered in the direction that God was taking me. No more tear stained pillows! My boots were on the ground! My spirit was strong, my eyes seeing beyond all doubt cast in front of me.

I took notes at every appointment and paid close attention. Writing down and asking questions, is a must! Being ORGANIZED is a must! My family was depending on me. I knew I had to be jack tough and double ready for whatever came my way! My life and the lives of my loved ones were worth the fight!

For he who is in you is Greater Than he who is in the World! 1 John 4:4.

Notes:

CONTINUE TO ABIDE

I received a phone call from my husband at work letting me know that he would be coming home early and was not feeling well. This was very odd considering my husband worked 10-12 hours a day, with a busy 2-hour round trip commute. Throughout our lives it was common for him to travel for business. I mean my God, I had to corner this man into taking his vacation time. He has a strong foundation as a leader, father, husband and human being. When it comes to taking care of people around him, he always made sure he was the last to eat. When he finally arrived home that day I met him in the driveway only to find fear in his eyes, his clothes & body soaked with sweat and his skin was that of hot coals. He was complaining of severe stomach pain and could barely walk! My gentle 6'7" 260 LB giant was for the 1st time in our lives.....VUNERABLE! I told him to put his arm over my shoulder so I could help him into the house. He took the 1st step and began vomiting profusely. He couldn't make it upstairs so I lied him on the sofa and covered him with multiple blankets because he said he was freezing. I put a cold cloth on his forehead and gave him Tylenol because his temperature rose to 105. I was unsure what to do, so I called the specialist's office and was told by the receptionist that she would send the Doctor a message and we should expect a call back. At the end of the day I received a call back from one of the nurse Practitioner's saying there was nothing that could be done, it was Friday as they were preparing to leave for the weekend. I explained to her how high his temperature was and I was feeling very concerned. The nurse practitioner said the only thing I could do was give him Tylenol and keep an eye on the fever. I could feel him slipping away to the fever as it rose to 107 at times. I could feel the presence of death in my bedroom that night. The sweetness of slumber never came to me that evening, I prayed throughout the night that God would spare him. I cared for him round the clock for the entire weekend. I had to wash and assist my husband in and out of bathroom. I guess this is the part where I'm supposed to feel alone and afraid. I was alone but I was determined that through the Grace of God, we would get through this. I felt so thankful that he lived through the weekend. I dressed him and brought him to the doctor's office without an appointment. One of the Nurse Practitioners came out into the waiting room, looked at him and then took his blood pressure and temperature. She turned to me and said I am not trying to scare you but he could die if you don't get him to the hospital, he could slip away in a matter of hours. She also advised me not to bring him back to the local hospital because they were not equipped to handle his condition. I told her I would bring him to the next city over. She said she would contact the Emergency room.

Once at the hospital he was admitted with sepsis, a critically high temperature, high kidney numbers, high liver numbers and bacterial pneumonia. In a nutshell he was in tough shape! It was a few weeks before returned home.

Notes:

NOT GIVING UP!

We had a follow up appointment with the specialist. He said the numbers were not good and once again started to talk about alcohol. He said I would send you to a transplant specialist but they won't touch you because of the addiction. At this time, I was very determined to continue to tell him this was not the case. He said well if it was something else we would be able to find it, if we looked for it. I said well that's good, then you should look for it. He appeared to be very annoyed with me and said well it could be hemochromatosis but I'm 100% sure it's not. Never the less I will look for a cause so we can stop with all this. My response was, when we find the real cause we should stop with all the other talk. He laughed and said I'm positive that's not the case. In that moment I held my tongue as I thanked God! I thought to myself, now we can finally look for the real cause!

Notes:

FINDING TRUTH

My husband had an appointment to surgically have a biopsy of his liver removed to find the true cause of his condition. We were informed there was so much fluid that his stomach had to be drained before a biopsy could be taken. During this time, we met a professional medical team who walked us through the entire procedure, every step of the way. I informed the team of his history as paperwork was read. It was brought to our attention that alcohol was the 1st, easiest and most common diagnosis, which is rarely validated. We were also informed it was good that the biopsy was being taken so we were able to know what the true cause was. My heart melted to look at the amount of fluid leaving his body, liter after liter being drained. I was really thankful the Doctor allowed me to stay in the room with my husband because he was so ill and fragile. My husband had lost a tremendous amount of weight. His appearance had significantly changed, most people would not recognize him. We have a history that will always be recognized and can never be forgotten. Toe Tags and Body Bags Forever my love......

Notes:

RESULTS ARE IN!

Finally, the day of truth! Not a day of opinion or feelings but the DAY OF TRUTH! My husband and I waited over an hour in the waiting room before being called into the exam room. We then waited about another hour before the specialist came in. When the Doctor came in, he stood leaning against the wall as he looked down at the floor. The Nurse Practitioner who accompanied him started reading results. She said although results did not show Hemochromatosis the results are not good because the report shows Alpha 1 Antitrypsin Deficiency. The Specialist continued to shake his head and say this is impossible. I just can't believe this. I have only treated 1 other person in my entire career for this. This is extremely rare! He just kept repeating impossible. I said Thank you God, we have found the cause. I know it's not a good report, but at least we can move forward. The specialist said at this time I will refer you to the transplant center and they will take it from here......... I could still hear him mumbling under his breath as he left the room "impossible, impossible"!

In hindsight, my experience as a caretaker, wife, and mother, has reinforced the need to research/review performance and social history on physicians prior to an appointment. Life is Precious!

Notes:

DRAINING PROCESS

My husband still dragged his dying body to work every day despite the fact that he now had to have a paracentesis done 1 to 2 times a week, removing anywhere from 10-12 liters of fluid each time from his stomach. Every time his stomach was drained he was 15 pounds lighter prior to the appointment. He was malnourished so none of his wardrobe fit and he was always dressed in layers to keep his bones warm. Dinner time wasn't the same because it never stayed down. Fevers, sweats, vomiting, severe stomach pain, and asities became the new norm and a shadow was cast over our dreams. Every day was a race against death as we waited for the appointment to be seen at the transplant center.

Notes:

I STAND AT THE DOOR

The transplant center was 1 ½ hours away which ended up being over 2 hours with traffic. When we arrived to the parking garage we bowed our heads and held hands in prayer. I felt the anointing of God as we walked through the front doors, pass the doormen, and then all the way up to the waiting room on the 6th floor. My husband's name was called, we stood together and walked down the long corridor to find the answers we had been seeking. Matthew 7:7-8 Ask, and it shall be given you; seek, and ye shall find; knock, and it shall be opened unto you: For every one that asketh receiveth; and he that seeketh findeth; and to him that knocketh it shall be opened. Amen!

When the Doctor entered the room, GREATNESS entered the room! The Doctor whom which we saw was very professional and extremely thorough. We were informed that he would have to run labs and follow up with his own findings. He needed to be absolutely sure this was Alpha 1. This was our 2nd opinion and we had to be certain. There was no doubt in mind, in fact I was absolutely certain that we were in the right place. The power of the holy spirit was in the midst of all doubt that had been put in front of us.

Ephesians 3:20-21 Now unto him that is able to do exceedingly abundantly above all that we ask or think, according to the power that worketh in us, Unto him be glory in the church by Christ Jesus throughout all ages, world without end. Amen.

There is no task to great for God! Never underestimate the power that is within us!

On the drive home, my husband looked at me and said I'm not entirely sure if I want a transplant. He said I need to understand what the quality of life is post-transplant. I refuse to be a burden on my family and I won't leave you alone and broke! I looked at him and said I don't care about the money! I'm not going to sugar coat this, I don't care if where living in the projects with a Mercedes parked out front, we'll just be ghetto fabulous and you'll be alive.

Notes:

RECOMMENDATIONS!

A conclusive diagnosis was made that my husband had Alpha 1 Antitrypsin. A liver transplant was recommended if he wanted to survive. We would have to attend classes and meet a series of requirements that were financial (insurance), medical (to make sure patient would be able to survive major surgery and ensure there were no other medical issues that needed to be addressed prior to), meet with social worker (to make sure patient has support through family/friends) and a dietician (to ensure the nutritional needs of the patient are met). This all had to be done before my husband's name could even go onto the waiting list to receive a liver. In addition to all of this the social worker noticed prior notes from the specialist pinpointing the medical condition to alcohol. Despite the fact my husband explained this was not the case, he was asked to attend an alcohol and drug assessment anyways to find out if there were any addictions. The assessment came back conclusive, clearing my husband of all alcohol and drug dependencies. We understood and respected that the transplant team had to make sure all concerns were looked into.

During this time my husband's health and appearance continued to decline, despite the odds I continued to trust and believe in God's promise. I believed my husband was in the right place with the right Doctors, I also knew that God never removed his hands from the situation.

Notes:

EMERGENCY

On this particular appointment day, it took me 2 ½ hours to get to the Transplant Center because of traffic. My husband was very weak and could barely walk. I drove up to the entrance and assisted him into the lobby. I then drove to the parking garage to find a spot so I could hurry back to get him upstairs and sign in at the front desk.

During the appointment I informed the Doctor that my husband's last meld score from the referring doctor was 27. He looked at me and said who told you that? Are you sure you don't mean 17 or 18! I don't think he would be standing here like this, most people would be in the hospital unable to function on a daily basis! I laughed to myself and thought my husband was always a tough nut to crack! The Doctor seemed genuinely concerned and said he will need to take labs at the end of the appointment to find out what his meld score was. Once the appointment was over, we headed to a nearby hotel because we had an early appointment the next day at the transplant center. My husband was feeling very sick which made it impossible for him or I to get any sleep that night. We miraculously arrived back to the transplant center early the next morning. The nurse coordinator confirmed that his meld score was a 27 as she walked us to the examination room. My husband was feeling very sick and had to use the restroom because he had to throw up. The emergency alarm went off in the bathroom that he was using. He apologized and said I was reaching for the wall so I wouldn't fall and pulled the emergency cord by accident. The Doctor admitted him into the hospital that day to try and stabilize him. Our daughter who lived 1 ½ hours away dropped everything to rush to her dad's side. I could see in my husband's eyes, that having our daughter there was the best medicine that could have been prescribed. We waited several hours anticipating tests results to come back to determine if he would have the medical clearance he needed to get listed for an organ. Finally, we were informed that my husband was being released and he had the medical clearance he needed to be listed. Our family was over joyed! After being released from the hospital, we gathered his belongings and started walking down the corridor until we heard the nurse calling my husband's name, as we turned the nurse was running toward us. We quickly walked to meet her halfway. She said I'm so sorry but I'm glad I caught you. The Doctor needs to speak with you before you leave. The Doctor informed us that one of the last tests came back and certain medical issues had to be resolved before he could go on the waiting list to receive an organ. This really wasn't what we wanted to hear but it's what we needed to know to survive the surgery. I thanked God that the transplant Doctors were making sure all issues were addressed before we went into this.

My husband was referred to a nephrologist because his kidney numbers continued to get worse. During the appointment the Doctor discussed there might be a possibility of a double transplant, both kidney and liver. This conversation seemed so surreal! Until now I didn't think I could hear anything worse. The Doctor was part of the transplant team, he was professional and very knowledgeable. Everything inside of me trusted him! He said in order to make a final determination, he would study his kidney numbers from the last 3 years and monitor his present kidney numbers. He needed to conclude that my husband had no kidney abnormalities prior to his liver diagnosis and also make sure the kidneys were healthy enough to improve post-transplant. I was really quiet on the drive home and that doesn't happen a lot. It was a good time to gather my thoughts and let go of negative energy!

The nephrologist eventually came to the determination that my husband did not need a double transplant and he gave him the medical clearance regarding his kidneys. Praise God!

We kept every appointment and followed all the instructions the transplant team gave us. The Doctors were determined to save my husband's life and I was certain to stay by his side believing it would come to pass.

Finally, after numerous appointments with multiple physicians it was determined that my husband would be able to have transplant surgery. The last step is for all of his information to be processed and presented to the board for a final approval.

The day came when we received a call letting us know that my husband was approved for his name to go onto the waiting list to receive an organ.

Notes:

DELIVERY PLAN

During the pre-transplant classes we were given literature and educated on what to expect post-transplant. We were informed that the patient would be seen early mornings, 2-3 times a week for several months at clinic. The clinic appointments will make it more successful for the patient to be monitored during this time. I decided to rent and furnish an apartment in the same city and state as the Transplant Center. I concluded that having an apartment close to where my husband would be having surgery and receiving aftercare would help us get through the process more successfully. This was the best decision I could have made for us. Everyone's situation is little different whether it is financial, travel, or distance to the transplant center. Sitting down and preplanning all concerns prior to surgery regarding children, pets, home etc. will help the surgery day and recovery time go smoother.

Notes:

A SWEET KISS WITH DEATH

By now my husband was on a cane and could not walk far distances. I found myself putting him into a wheel chair to get him from the lobby to his appointments. His body was malnourished and he could barely hold his head up. He was disabled and unable to function, he had to take a temporary leave from work as his condition rapidly deteriorated. I am a true visionary and have always been able to see ahead, never did I imagine I would find myself assisting my gentle giant with the simple daily tasks of bathing and dressing. At this time my husband's meld score reached an all-time high of 30. He was still having 1-2 paracentesis a week. I could taste death on his lips as I kissed him every night before bed. I embraced death in my arms every evening, I knew if I let go there would be no return for my soulmate. I captured each moment of bitterness and returned it with a sweet melody of love. Our long intimate nights were replaced by sickness and the stench of death that made the air in our bedroom somehow unbreathable. I felt unbreakable with the determination of love! I would carry him on my back if I had to! As I looked through spiritual eyes at every obstacle in front of me, I could foresee us getting a phone call to receive his new organ. It was just a matter of time!

Notes:

THE CALL

On this day we decided to leave the apartment for a few days and head back to our home. It seemed like a long day getting my husband ready and packing the pets back up. Once home I got us situated and then we retired for the evening. For the 1st time in a while I fell into a deep sleep. In the wee hours the phone rang, I jumped up! It was a nurse from the transplant center informing us there was an organ match for my husband and it was a good liver. They needed to know how long it would take us to get there. We were also informed there was another patient at a different hospital that was ahead of him to receive the organ, if for any reason he/she could not receive the organ it would then go to my husband. I got us ready as quickly as I could, packed the pets back up and headed out. Once at the apartment I told my husband to wait in the car because he couldn't walk on his own. I then tended to the pets or the boys as we call them with food and water etc., then raced back down stairs to drive to the hospital.

When we arrived at the hospital, I pulled up to the front and tried to assist him out of the car. He was literally at the end that night and I couldn't get him out of the car by myself. I went inside to the front desk where there were 3 women working. I gave them my name, my husband's name and informed them my husband was there for an organ transplant. I asked if there was someone to assist me getting him out of the car into a wheel chair because I couldn't budge him. The three women looked at me and one of them replied no! They continued with their conversation as if I were a nuisance. I didn't understand as I was the only person in the lobby in the wee hours. Never the less I said OK, I was determined to go back and get him by myself, in that moment the security guard sitting to the side said excuse me Ma'am but did you say what I think you said, that your husband is here to receive an organ. I said yes Sir. He said I will help you get him into a wheelchair. I thanked him so much as he assisted my husband into the chair. Once inside one of the women from the front desk called and assisted us upstairs to the 10th tower. I thanked her over and over again despite the poor treatment we received initially. There was no time for worrying about things we had no control over. Something awesome was about to take place!

Notes:

WE HAVE ARRIVED

This was the big day we had hoped and prayed for. My husband was admitted and a series of tests were done to make sure this was a good match. The 1st nurse said let's keep our fingers crossed and hopefully he receives the organ because sometimes that's not always the case. Shortly after, another nurse who watched us being admitted, came into the room, shut the door and asked if she could pray with us. We replied yes. We held hands and believed in the almighty name of God! On the way out, she said I am heading out soon but in the name of Jesus, he is showing me that you will receive this transplant. The next person to walk through the door was our daughter as we were touched by the love and support she showed. Finally, the Surgeon came in and said we have a liver and it belongs to you, if you still want it. In that moment our family filled the room with tears of joy. The Surgeon's voice was calming and reassuring as he walked us through what would take place. After the Surgeon left the room, the nurse who prayed with us came to the doorway and lifted her hands in praise. My husband and I never said a word we just smiled and lifted our hands back!

Our daughter and I were able to stay with my husband right until he was taken into surgery. He was given lots of love, hugs and kisses.... See you Soon Daddy!

I carried two UNC Basketballs around in a bag so that each surgeon, nurse and all medical staff members would be able to sign the balls. We anticipated a great beginning to our story, we will always remain humble and grateful to the donor. May God bless their family and bring comfort to their hearts. Amen!

If you're reading this please prepare yourself for a long emotional waiting period during the surgical procedure. My daughter and I did a lot of praying and reflecting on our lives together as a family. We talked about funny things and weird moments. The surgery alone was over 6 hours. We were kept up to date on his condition throughout the entire process, which was amazing.

When the surgery was over my daughter and I were called into a consultation room to speak with the Surgeon who performed the transplant surgery. The surgery was successful and my husband was doing very well. He said thirteen liters of fluid had to be removed before the surgery began. He was still in the surgical area for observation and would be brought up to ICU where our daughter and I would be able to see him. The surgeon reminded us that he would not be alert and still heavily sedated. He was professional and somehow empathetic toward the situation at the same time. I thank God, every day for the doctors, surgeons and medical staff that helped save my husband's life. I can't say it enough, thank God for the Transplant Team.

As my daughter and I walked into the ICU to see my husband, he had multiple tubes and IV's and was still heavily sedated. We held each other as we stood by his bedside. It was getting into the late evening hours. We met his male nurse who was caring and very professional. He was very informative and answered all of our questions. He made sure he had our contact information and reassured me that my husband would be well cared for. Our daughter and I prayed by his bedside and blew kisses on the way out. His nurse called when we arrived back to the apartment to let us know that he understood how concerned we were. He said please feel welcome to call with any questions or concerns. I felt God's favor all around us. It was a full 24 hours without any sleep, and I still had to walk the dog at 1am. I knew if I didn't get any sleep it would turn into a full 48 hours. I tried to force myself to sleep but I couldn't, instead I laid there with my eyes closed for 2-3 hours so I could get back to ICU ASAP. I had to be there when my gentle giant woke up. I wanted him to know his family was right there by his side.

Notes:

T10

The next morning, our daughter and I arrived bright and early at the hospital. We were pleasantly surprised to find him alert and doing well. I stood there smiling as the medical staff surrounded his bed, they listened to him tell stories of his college years playing basketball. This was the after moment! This was God's promise being fulfilled right before our eyes! Amen!

The biggest challenge was the amount of fluid that continued to drain from his stomach. It was a lot of work for the nurses to tend to.

On the third day, he was moved from ICU to the tenth tower, which was known as T10. He was encouraged to walk a few times a day to gain strength. He was on a high protein diet because he needed to concentrate on weight gain. His room was filled with his 2 favorite girls. Family, love and support is the best medicine anyone could use at a time like this.

I was there bright and early, every morning before the transplant team arrived to do their morning rounds. Our daughter's daily presence, funny sense of humor and amazing never-ending stories kept a smile on our faces. She compared his scar to a Thug Life tattoo from a music video. To Funny! Our daughter was truly a well diverse young woman who attended school in 6 different states of which 3 were during her high school years. She was the most nonjudgmental, loving young ladies that I have ever known. She was our Moonpie and I loved her with every bone in my body.

On the 6th day I arrived on T10 with Starbucks coffee to find my husband showered with his bath robe over his Johnny. He was smiling as he said I've already gone 8 laps this morning. He said hurry up we don't want to be late for the meeting. I looked at him and said what meeting! He started walking out the door saying hurry up, as he pushed his IV that was clipped to a walking pole with wheels. Oh Boy I thought! I followed him to the end of the corridor to find the medical staff having an early morning meeting. Leave it to my husband, he was the only patient there. My husband's name was called out by the lead nurse, he then walked to the front of the group, introduced himself and pointed me out in the crowd as his wife. He began to tell his story and how thankful he was for everyone on the medical staff. After the meeting we were approached by numerous staff members, who said they had never been so privileged to hear anyone's story in such great detail. Staff members also expressed that after listening to my husband's story they felt they had the best job on the planet. This is the man that I married and chose to spend the rest of my life with. He is a man that motivates and brings people together. I felt so blessed and spiritually quenched that morning!

On day 7 my husband was released from the hospital with instructions for his prescriptions and follow up visits. The transplant team was highly organized and very reassuring. When it came to his aftercare we were in great hands.

On T-10 there is a bell on the wall that all patients ring after transplant on the day of release. His nurse and medical staff cheered on, as my husband sounded the bell on the way out of T-10! Ding, Ding, Ding, what a victorious sound as we headed onto new pastures!

Notes:

THE FALL

My husband had an early morning clinic appointment a few weeks after his surgery to have his staples removed. His name was called so he could have labs done before the appointment. When he started to walk through the door the lab tech's foot was in front of the pathway. Unfortunately, my husband ended up having a very bad fall because of it.

There was a lot of commotion in the waiting area and he was finally helped up from the floor and assisted to the back room in an office chair that had wheels to have his staples removed. After the staples were removed he was then assisted to a clinic wheelchair to have x-rays done. The x-rays did not show any broken bones. I then wheeled him down to the lobby and assisted him back into the car with the help of the lobby staff. When we arrived back to the apartment I realized that getting him out of the car, across a parking garage, to the elevator and down a long corridor to get back to the apartment was not planned out. I was able to get him out of the car, across the parking garage onto the elevator. Once we got off the elevator he was in so much pain I couldn't move him. There was no one local to call and it had taken me well over an hour just to get him this far. I put him against the wall as he leaned on my shoulder. We stood there for another 30 minutes as I tried to help/convince him that I could get us back to the apartment. My pep talk didn't change the situation. I told him that we should rest a minute. I wasn't sure what I was going to do, so I began to pray. In that moment a neighbor was walking to the elevator dressed in business attire. He asked if we were OK and I said no, I really need help getting him down the hall into the apartment. I could tell he was in a hurry, but without question or hesitation he said I'll help you. Thank God, he was able to lift my husband, get him down the long corridor, into the apartment then onto the sofa. I thanked him so much. I even offered him money. He said your welcome and refused the money. I really wasn't accustomed to asking or receiving help from others. God sent me an Angel! Never underestimate the kindness of others. Let this be a lesson to all, "Always overestimate the kindness you show others"!

A few days after the fall an appointment was made for my husband to see a specialist since he was still in a great deal of pain. After 2 ½ hours of waiting to be seen, a nurse came out and said if there is anyone that just got here we need to reschedule your appointment, if you have been waiting for 2 to 3 hours it could take up to another hour, so if you would like to reschedule that's fine too. My patience remained thick because my husband was in great deal of pain and really needed to be seen. We were finally seen by the Doctor after waiting another hour. To make a long story short and messy we were scheduled with a spine specialist who does not specialize in this type of injury. There was nothing he could do except refer us back to the transplant team. I laughed to myself and thought mistakes are made every day and there was no time to sweat the small stuff. Although finding crutches for a 6'7" person became a treasure hunt, I eventually found a pair, but that's another story. There were so many struggling moments that week! I could barely keep up!

The next day my husband was seen in clinic for one of his weekly appointments. His transplant specialist concluded it was best that he was put in the hospital because of the fall to determine the severity of the injury and ensure no harm was done to the transplant. While in the hospital his scans determined there was no harm done to his transplant but he suffered a fracture because of the fall. On top of everything that had occurred from the injury he still had a significant amount of ascites that was being monitored and drained as well.

All of this was taking place at the same time that he should be walking to gain strength. This was not the way his recovery was supposed to go. We had to be at the clinic at least two times a week, early mornings for multiple appointments. I stayed strong in prayer and followed any and all instructions the transplant team gave me. I trusted God and God entrusted me to his finest, the Transplant Team. I knew that things would get better and one day we would reflect back on this day. Weeping may endure for a night, but joy cometh in the morning (Psalm 30:5).

Notes:

REJECTION

I was faced with so many obstacles at this time. My husband was not getting better and still had a significant amount of ascites. On this particular day we left the apartment to head back home, as soon as we walked through the door we received a phone call from the transplant nurse informing us of his last labs. The nurse said my husband needed to be put back into the hospital immediately because his organ was in rejection. Once again, I had to turn right back around to drive out of state to get him to the hospital. The transplant team would monitor and stabilize his condition. The team surgeon said we have never lost a liver to rejection. Through the power of prayer and the profound knowledge of the team of Surgeons and Doctors my husband was discharged to continue his recovery. Jehovah Rapha! The God I serve is a healer!

Notes:

RELENTLESS CHALLENGES

A couple of months had gone by and once again my husband was feeling very ill. He was fatigued, lethargic, high fevers and had a loss of appetite. We also had other personal affairs going on at this time as well. We had 2 hail storms that destroyed the entire roof of our home and damaged one of the vehicles. I was also having issues with the company that we hired to replace the roof.

When it rains it pours and so did my daily challenges! My pug was diagnosed with pancreatitis and hospitalized, he was also later diagnosed with high liver enzymes and his numbers were being closely watched at each appointment. At some point I thought we were headed in the right direction and then my fury little boy was injured in the back room at a Vet appointment, he suffered a torn ACL while having his nails trimmed by a technician. It was a horrible experience and he suffered a great deal of pain during this time. He couldn't get around by himself, so I found myself carrying his 30lb butt everywhere. I loved him and would make sure I did everything in my power to help nurse him back to walking condition. He eventually was able to walk again but was never quite the same with jumping and running. His emotional scars never healed, as the painful experience followed him to each vet appointment. I'm happy to say at the end of the day he is still loving and faithful with his family. Although his walks are just a little shorter, he still enjoys them along with lots of belly rubs. Lord give me strength!

At this time in my life everything I did came back to me 10-fold with a dark return. I couldn't catch a break! The harder I prayed the worse things got. I had an advantage over the situation of unfortunate events that continued to come my way! I could see with spiritual eyes that understanding Ephesians 6:12 - For we wrestle not against flesh and blood, but against principalities, against powers, against the rulers of the darkness of this world, against spiritual wickedness in high places. Preparing ourselves with Ephesians 6:13 – Wherefore take unto you the whole armour of God, that ye maybe able to withstand in the evil day, and having done all to stand.

It's not about how hard times get, it's about how hard we get up and roll during those adverse times! We can't fight fire with fire but we all understand that water will put out the fire!

I was able to stand with a clear view of the elements that plagued my situation. Being able to shield yourself in dark times doesn't mean you're the strongest person, it means you're well prepared to withstand the blows, at the same time possessing the wisdom on how to reciprocate. I knew my enemies plans before they were put into play!

Let's face it, no one chooses Alpha 1 Antitrypsin deficiency, I don't know anyone who stands in line for cancer, or picks out Lupus for their loved ones. We might not always have the luxury of picking and choosing our battles, but one thing is for sure, the power of prayer, belief, and positive thinking combined, has given me authority over forces I had never imagined. At the end of the day 2 Chronicles 20:15 let's us know the battle is not ours, it belongs to God.

To my readers going through difficult times, understand that you might not think you're the smartest person or the most influential individual, you might even believe you can't get through your present situation because you don't see an exit! Sometimes there is no exit, so we have to go through it. No matter how tough it gets, you can always lean on God and he will protect and shield you and your family! He will see you through, no matter how ugly it looks, keep praying and believing. The best is yet to come! Amen!

Despite the way my husband felt physically he talked about being able to return to work on a daily basis. We were reassured by the company that he did not need to worry about his position, it would be there when he was able to return. What a blessing to have a billion-dollar company supporting our family in the darkest time we have ever faced. Once again, more challenges were presented to us in the form of a phone call from his employer. His employer wanted him to know that his position could no longer be held open because his role was so critical to the company. My husband was still severely ill and fighting to recover. I stood there speechless in disbelief. I was able to see with a spiritual eye that we can't always control 100% of what happens to us but most importantly we can control 100% on how we deal with adversity.

During this time of dealing with so much in our lives, the transplant team discovered that my husband's continued sickness was caused by an infection from the transplant surgery. My husband was put on medication and closely watched. This went on for months until the infection was finally cleared. By now the holidays were upon us and the only thing I wanted for Christmas couldn't be gift wrapped.

God walked and talked to me on a daily basis. Strange as it may sound, he even spoke through me to comfort others whom I met at the hospitals and clinics. Maybe it was just a warm smile or a listening ear. You don't always have to scream brimstone and fire down people's throats, sometimes people just need the human side cared for. Scripture tells us he will never leave us nor forsake us. He has kept his word to me. I, Anna Wilkison am a witness and follower for the teachings of our Lord and Savior Jesus Christ.

Notes:

KEEPING THE FAITH

Finally, things were moving in the right direction until my husband started waking up with different joints of his body severely swelled. The best way to describe the swelling was like a water balloon being taped to a person's elbow or knee. It was beet red and I had never seen anything like it. The pain was debilitating and unbearable to touch. At one point he could not use his arm or put pressure on one of his legs, as he had to use crutches to walk. The transplant specialist recommended we see his primary care physician. We had multiple appointments with his primary care physician, who was uncertain on his condition. The swelling and condition was sporadic and inconsistent in various parts of the body, as this continued on for long periods. He had to take pain killers just to get dressed. Eventually the primary care physician referred him to a specialist who could not see him for at least 9 months. There was no way he could continue to function in this condition. I called every day to see if there were any cancellations. We were blessed to get a last-minute spot on a cancellation appointment. The specialist examined and evaluated my husband and found his condition was induced by medication. My husband was then able to be treated successfully.

I was convinced at this point nothing else could happen and without warning my husband ended up with a bad case of shingles. One more milestone before receiving the ultimate Crown!

Once again, we are thankful for the knowledge of modern medicine and God's divine intervention. All of this seems so surreal that two people could face so many obstacles and still find a way not to give up because of the power of prayer. Hebrews 11:1 Faith is the substance of things hoped for, the evidence of things not seen...

Notes:

MY EXPERIENCE WITH DISABILITY, LIFE AND MEDICAL INSURANCE

Disability Insurance: Every obstacle we faced was met with relentless piles of paper work and phone calls from the disability insurance, which made it next to impossible for my husband to recover comfortably. The Doctors notes were questioned line by line. In an effort to be proactive and prevent any issues with coverage we felt the pressure to review Doctor's notes and labs through the patient portal to prevent any unjust denial of benefits. There were always ongoing failures to respond to communication and repetitive requests for redundant information.

Life Insurance: I tried to get a private life insurance post-transplant for my husband and discovered that it is next to impossible after an individual has been transplanted. If you have Private Life Insurance before the transplant then you cannot be kicked off post-transplant, but you will not be able to increase the amount of coverage. If you did not have private life insurance before the transplant then there are two options after transplant that we were made aware of: Option 1 is a single premium whole life policy called an estate maximizer, using this example: Put down 15,000 and get 34,000 at the time of death. Option 2 is an annuity (basically a high yield savings account). If the individual is able to return to work then they would be able to receive life insurance through their employer.

Considering my husband's life insurance policies have always been in the $1 million plus range and changed to 0 after his employment ended, has given me the desire to encourage everyone who is planning on having a transplant to find out what their options are prior to.

The Medical insurance: Our medical Insurance went into Cobra and the premiums were significantly higher. Since we were satisfied with coverage we kept the Cobra coverage for as long as we were allowed because it was well worth it. Everyone's situation/finances are different. Make sure you do your research and compare costs. Make sure you understand the full scope of your medical benefits. Be sure to ask about catastrophic benefits before you have a transplant, you might be surprised on what it covers (meals, lodging, travel etc.).

Overall, I always felt grateful for rainy days because it prepared us for the ultimate storm. By no means were we rich or owned a hedge fund. We just did some good planning early on in our lives. Remember no matter where you find yourself with finances there is a way to plan ahead and make it through the most adverse times of your life. We are all in God's Hands!

Notes:

THE BEGINNING

After everything I went through during this time, I felt a piece of my core was missing. The feeling was so strong as if I woke up without hands, feet, or vision. I prayed for an understanding and God revealed to me there was a piece of Anna missing. The piece that was missing was no longer needed, it was the unnecessary part that stood in the way of being the woman that God designed me to fully be. The forces that were trying to tear me down were being built back up brick by brick by God himself! God has reinforced me! I am Jack tough and double ready for whatever comes my way. I see with spiritual eyes! I hear God's voice through his teachings. My foot steps are ordered through the power of prayer!

Today is a new day and we are moving forward to new pastures. My husband is Physically, emotionally and spiritually feeling the healing and anointing of God! Our Lord and Savior has restored the body and mind to new endeavors! He has replaced death with the gift of life!

Remember stay Jack tough and double ready! Your life and the lives of your loved ones are worth the fight! Much Love....Anna

About the Author

A success story of a dedicated wife and mother. Anna Maria was born in the cold month of February, North of Boston, in Lowell Massachusetts, also known as Mill City, Murder Mills etc. One of the toughest little cities in the North East.

Anna has always had a David vs. Goliath warrior mentality, which has given her the strength to never back down when faced with numerous life challenges. She has never been led by the majority, but always driven by the minority. She has always been and will forever remain subservient to her greatest love "Family"! Anna has been called by God Almighty to shine a light of hope to those in times of darkness.

This book was written to give each reader the strength and belief that there is a warrior in each of us.

Out of the darkness of sorrow came a light of hope, reaching those in broken places...... Anna Maria Wilkison

Made in the USA
Lexington, KY
14 August 2018